SENT

Youth Study Book

SENT
Delivering the Gift of Hope at Christmas

Book

978-1-501-80103-7

978-1-501-80104-4 eBook

Devotions for the Season

978-1-501-80117-4

978-1-501-80118-1 eBook

DVD

978-1-501-80108-2

Leader Guide

978-1-501-80106-8

978-1-501-80107-5 eBook

Youth Study Book

978-1-501-80114-3

978-1-501-80115-0 eBook

Children's Leader Guide

978-1-501-80116-7

For more information, visit www.AbingdonPress.com

SENT

DELIVERING
THE GIFT OF HOPE
AT CHRISTMAS

JORGE ACEVEDO

with Jacob Armstrong, Rachel Billups, Justin LaRosa & Lanecia Rouse

Youth Study Book
by Kevin Alton

Abingdon Press
Nashville

Sent: Youth Study Book
Delivering the Gift of Hope at Christmas

Youth Study Book
by Kevin Alton

This book is printed on elemental chlorine-free paper.

ISBN 978-1-5018-0114-3

15 16 17 18 19 20 21 22 23 24—10 9 8 7 6 5 4 3 2 1
MANUFACTURED IN THE UNITED STATES OF AMERICA

CONTENTS

INTRODUCTION

Advent has a big job to do.

In the season of Advent, we wait and prepare for the coming of the Christ Child. We do have the distinct advantage of knowing that the Christ Child already came. Having the birth of Jesus noted at a specific point on our calendars, we back up four weeks and rejoice and watch and wait. Because we know it's going to happen.

A big part of what we're trying to experience during Advent, though, is the less certain waiting and longing experienced by the Jewish people who watched in anticipation for *centuries* without their hopes being realized. It's no wonder there was confusion about what was expected of the eventual Messiah. A few hundred years of "not yet" didn't exactly build clarity of a vision for the future. The prophets of old spoke out about deliverance from their oppressors, but the scattered kingdoms of Judah and Israel weren't even being oppressed by the same people by the time Jesus came along.

Jesus, on the other hand, seemed to know exactly what he was doing. As we watch him grow from a heralded infant into a committed spiritual child and eventually into a countercultural adult teacher and leader, it quickly becomes clear that Jesus didn't just happen—Jesus was *sent* with a purpose.

This knowledge that Jesus was sent imbues his every moment with significance, right from the beginning. This book explores Jesus' being sent to reconcile, to set us free, to be with us, to bring us new life, and to change everything. Jesus' presence on earth also invites us to take part in that wonderful movement of God in the world, because we too are sent, for all those same reasons. We are invited in Advent to prepare our hearts for participation in bringing God's kingdom—on earth, as it is in heaven.

To the Leader

The chapters of this book are related to the chapters of an adult resource called *Sent: Delivering the Gift of Hope at Christmas*. The content varies between the two books, but they share a focus text and theme, which should allow for some common conversation wherever your youth interact with adult groups.

Each chapter begins with a section exploring the themes and Scriptures from the adult resource, with examples from my own family and ministry experiences.

Going Deeper

Here you'll find three additional devotional thoughts using Scripture that complements the main text for the chapter. If you're using this book with a group, a helpful approach would be to have group members commit to completing the reading and devotions before coming together as a group.

Making It Personal

These are some reflective thoughts and questions that look back over the texts and themes and are intended to be answered alone. If you've completed the devotions during the week, it might be helpful to look over these questions right before you go to meet with your group. If you're not meeting with a group, you can use them whenever you like.

Sharing Thoughts and Feelings

These group questions can serve as an icebreaker to open your group time together. They should also allow anyone who hasn't read to be drawn in to the conversation.

Doing Things Together

Each chapter concludes with two fifteen-minute activities designed to engage your group with the material in a new way. Supplies are minimal, but be sure that someone is in charge of bringing everything necessary to the experience. Most of the activities wrap up with one or two additional discussion questions or a peek back at the text.

Listening for God

In this section you'll find a closing prayer.

Blessings to you on your journey through Advent as you discover how Christ was sent and how we in turn are sent.

1.

JESUS RECONCILES

In that region there were shepherds living in the fields, keeping watch over their flock by night. Then an angel of the Lord stood before them, and the glory of the Lord shone around them, and they were terrified. But the angel said to them, "Do not be afraid; for see—I am bringing you good news of great joy for all the people." (Luke 2:8-10 NRSV)

In the Dead of Night

I don't remember the age it happened for him, but it was magical.

The realization was almost too much for Grey, my oldest son, who probably was four or five years old at the time. Waffle House was open *all night*. He couldn't believe it. He just couldn't get over the idea that while he slept, other people were *beginning* their day—working through the night, serving food to people. The concept became an onion his little mind was set on de-layering. "What about their families? Do mommies work at Waffle Houses? Who's *eating* in the middle of the night?"

I promised him that—some day, eventually—we'd go in the middle of the night so he could see for himself. Obviously making such an excursion would take either solid, intentional planning or an unreasonable collision of unlikely circumstances. I chose to wait for the latter.

Fast-forward three years. Grey, then seven or eight, still had not been to a Waffle House in the middle of the night. Nor had Penner, his brother, who was two years younger. At that point in our lives, my wife and I both worked for a local church, where I served as director of youth ministries and she as director of children's ministries. That January, we had continuing education events that overlapped. Grandparents covered the parenting gap, and when I returned, Granddaddy picked me up at the airport, boys in tow.

Exhausted, I headed to bed soon after the boys that night. I was glad to be home and even more grateful to be in my own bed. Sleeping. Ahhhhhhh.

"Dad. Dad."

"What...what on earth, Grey," I mumbled.

"I had a bad dream. Can I watch TV?"

I wriggled around trying to find a clock to consult. No glasses on. Useless. So I said, "What time is it, anyway?"

He pat-patted away to the kitchen and then came back. "It's 3:08 a.m.," he informed me.

"No, Grey, go back to bed. That's nuts. It's the middle of the night."

My words echoed in my head. *It's the middle of the night.* Stupid promises. It's the middle of the night. Mom is out of town. Waffle House is open.

Darn it. I couldn't *not* do it.

My words came in an exhausted rush. "It's the middle of the night and Mom's not here, so we can probably go to Waffle House if you want to, but we have to ask your brother because if he doesn't want to go it would be mean waking him up, and we can't go without him. Okay?" I sucked in one of those long, high-pressure yawns.

"Okay," Grey said.

I went to Penner's bed, hoping against hope that he would decline the invitation.

"Penner. *Penner.*" Maybe he wouldn't even wake up. "Penner."

He squeezed up his eyes and wrinkled his nose, a customary first response.

"Penner, it's the middle of the night. Do you want to go to Waffle House and get a waffle in the middle of the night?" I was overexplaining it, but it was the best I could manage at the time. He scrunched up his nose again. Maybe he would just fall back asleep.

"Yyyyeesssss," he exhaled.

So we loaded up a three-way jammies party and headed into town.

As you might imagine, there's not a much cuter sight than two little boys in their pj's in the middle of the night at a Waffle House, so there was no shortage of conversation. All the wait staff came by to talk. We got to meet a handful of truck drivers and factory workers. The experience was otherworldly for both the boys and me. We'd stepped into a time and place that wasn't our own and had glimpsed a different way of life.

As we drove home, Grey leaned his head against the seat and closed his eyes. A few minutes later, I heard him quietly say, "Dad?"

"Yes, Grey?"

"I'd like to go back and visit the night people again sometime."

Every now and then, we do.

Come to Reconcile

Even when I was a kid I wondered why Jesus was born in the middle of the night. That curiosity did not subside after having two children of my own, each heavily involving the middle of the night in their births. You'd think that if anybody could be born at a convenient hour it would be Jesus. Even if it was just as a courtesy to Mary—"Hey, sorry about the surprise pregnancy; let's put you up in a nice hotel and have the birth around brunch. Sound good?" Nope. Middle of the night.

But God was coming to bring things back together—to reconcile.

Fitting, then, to announce the coming Christ Child in the middle of the night. The angels appeared to the overnight shepherds; honor enough. How exciting, to be among the first to be in Jesus' presence! But imagine the people who approached them in the coming days—if you wanted to hear more about that middle-of-the-night miracle, you'd have to seek out the "night people."

Just as Jesus came to reconcile, we are called to join in that work of reconciliation. Fortunately, the real work of reconciliation is done by God, but we have a great role of inviting people into that relationship. Not a hard-nosed accept-or-reject invitation, but a relational coming-alongside invitation. Just being in community with other people allows your life to offer God's love in the lives of others.

An example of that, once again courtesy of Waffle House:

It was Christmas Eve. I was at the home of my girlfriend Britta's family, not too long before we would be married. We were watching a movie, when suddenly Britta's brother Pete asked, "When are we going to Waffle House?"

Everyone exchanged glances. "Why would we go to Waffle House?"

Pete said, "We *always* go to Waffle House on Christmas Eve!"

The conversation went back and forth. Pete was increasingly agitated, now pacing. The fact was, it was at least my fifth Christmas Eve spent with Britta's family, and in that time we'd *never* gone to Waffle House. Eventually, though, to appease Pete, we loaded up and headed out for waffles.

It immediately became a family tradition (or continued an existing one, depending on who you ask). Even with our families scattered apart by a few hours' drive, we manage most years to land at a Waffle House somewhere on Christmas Eve.

The meal has a feeling of reconciliation—reaching out to spend time with night people who are separated from their families on a holiday. Some are there for the extra holiday pay. Some are there because they don't have family to visit. Whatever the reason, there's a feeling of community in a place where usually there isn't.

I wonder if the shepherds sensed some of that community on the first Christmas.

Going Deeper

Opportunity Lost

Moses is a hero of Scripture, a clear leader among leaders. He was sent by God to bring the Israelites out of slavery and into the freedom that God desired for them. After a close encounter with death as an infant, Moses found himself raised in Pharaoh's palace, primed to be a key figure in leadership. At the age of forty, he decided to visit his own people—where everything suddenly went wrong.

Read Acts 7:17-28. Keep in mind that this all happened *before* God met Moses in the desert.

- At the moment he was confronted about killing the Egyptian, what emotions do you think Moses experienced?
- How do you think your own actions affect the perception of others?
- When have your actions complicated your ability to offer reconciliation to others?
- Have you ever struggled to be reconciled to someone because of his or her actions? How can you always be ready to offer or receive reconciliation?

Come Together

During Advent, we yearn for the reconciliation that drew us to God in the first place. In the Wesleyan tradition, that yearning is called *prevenient grace*—the grace that goes before, drawing us to God before we're even aware of the source of our longing.

Read Ephesians 2:13-16.

We're familiar with the idea that God comes to reconcile; in fact, since you're reading this, there's a fair chance you've been raised with that story. The storyline often focuses on the coming together of humanity and God, which is true and wonderful. But the verses you just read indicate that another reconciliation takes place first: "both groups into one" in verse 14 (NRSV) refers to the blending of Jews (God's people) and Gentiles (everyone else) into one—all boundaries removed, humanity united.

- How does the way you live out your faith work to include others and not exclude them?

Everything in Its Place

At this point in your life, you've probably got a lot of people who are in charge of you at one time or another. Parents at home. Teachers at school. The coaches and other extracurricular leaders who are an increasingly important presence in the lives of youth. It's easy for the notion of "following Jesus" to fall to second place in our lives, and quickly. Then third. Eventually discipleship is a distant, dim wish.

Read Colossians 1:15-20.

- Where does God figure in your day-to-day life? Is your relationship with God a must or something you keep meaning to work on?
- What things would you have to give away in order for Christ truly to be your "head"?
- How does God's supremacy in your life (or lack of it) affect your ability to work for reconciliation in the world around you?

Making It Personal

One of the wonderful things about following the church calendar is that each time the seasons roll around, they present new opportunities for spiritual change and growth in our relationship with God. This is not to make excuses for the way we continually fall away, but we certainly can be grateful for the calendar's reminders of God's grace in our lives.

This Advent, be open to where God may be nudging you toward better relationships. What changes can you make that would

- increase your depth of discipleship?
- make you more familiar with Scripture?
- bring you closer to God in prayer?
- increase your confidence in letting God work through you in your community?

You're currently cruising toward the popular good-intentions trap of New Year's resolutions; don't let *this* become *that*. But—without serious dedication—all the good thinking you just did can wither away to nothing in terms of real change in your life. Write down some goals related to the answers you just gave to the above questions. Share the goals with friends who will keep you accountable, in love.

Sharing Thoughts and Feelings

Spend some time with the group discussing these questions:

- Jesus was sent to earth to reconcile. What do you think that means?
- Can you share an example of a time when you were able to reconcile with someone after suffering a serious hurt? Is there a situation in your life that you are still waiting to see reconciled?
- What are some ways we can be reconcilers for God?
- What hurts exist in your community that need reconciliation? (See "A Time to Heal," below.)
- Can you share a time you felt included when you didn't expect to be? How can we include others in what we're trying to accomplish with God?

Doing Things Together

Do Unto Others

Supplies: Contractor-grade trash bags, transportation

The season of Advent is a time when we're invited to prepare ourselves spiritually for the coming of Jesus. Unfortunately, it's also a time when our consumer culture hits maximum overdrive in its annual shopping frenzy. Find time to form a relationship with a local shelter or nonprofit resale shop. Work with them to determine what needs they face through the holiday season in terms of food or clothing donations.

Have your church group develop a plan for advertising a food and clothing drive in your community. Be as specific as possible in your requests. The shop may work a season ahead and might be looking for spring clothing rather than winter clothing. When you're trying to meet needs, it's important to actually find out what the needs are.

Establish drop-off and pickup points and an ending date. Some people may be willing to donate ahead of Christmas, but others may want to wait until after. If your group is willing, form a relationship (we're reconciling, remember?) with that charity or shelter. What other things can you do together to help reach your community?

A Time to Heal

Supplies: Honesty

This activity will probably be a little different from anything your church group may have done: you're going to dig up an old hurt and try to heal it.

Work together to remember an unresolved, difficult issue that was faced by your group, church, or community. This could be between two or more people, families, or schools, and it could involve any interaction that ended bitterly or was unsettled. If you pick an unresolved issue within your peer group, consider bringing in a trusted adult or two to help moderate.

When you've identified the hurt, talk through these questions:

- Who was hurt in this instance?
- What was done at the time to try to heal?
- After the situation had died down a little, what happened to the parties involved?

Spend some time talking about what your group could do to offer some healing in that situation. What would be the best path to reconciliation? Has enough time passed that peaceful conversation can take place?

Whether or not you carry through with your plan, reflect on these questions:

- What were your immediate feelings when this activity was described?
- What can make reconciliation difficult between two people or groups?
- How do you see God's reconciling love working in your life?

Listening for God

God, may we fully participate in your reconciling work in this world! Thank you for sending Jesus to bring your creation back into relationship with you. Amen.

2.

JESUS SETS US FREE

Jesus went to Nazareth, where he had been raised. On the Sabbath he went to the synagogue as he normally did and stood up to read. The synagogue assistant gave him the scroll from the prophet Isaiah. He unrolled the scroll and found the place where it was written:

> *The Spirit of the Lord is upon me,*
>   *because the Lord has anointed me.*
> *He has sent me to preach good news to the poor,*
>   *to proclaim release to the prisoners*
>   *and recovery of sight to the blind,*
>   *to liberate the oppressed,*
>   *and to proclaim the year of the Lord's favor.*
>   *(Luke 4:16-19 CEB)*

A Deafening Silence

When you grow up in the church, it's easy to get used to certain things during a church service. Over time you realize you're no longer processing (much less singing) the last hymn—you're thinking about lunch. You tune in here and there during the Scripture, but a lot of times your brain says, "Scripture: check," and you move on to whatever is next in the service. You're usually good for at least the first five minutes of the sermon, or until you've decided if (a) it's interesting or (b) you've heard it before.

To tell the truth, it's rare that we're genuinely *surprised* in church. A sermon on giving? Oh, surprise. A story about a preacher making a home visit? Color me interested. Perhaps the greatest irony is checking out mentally during an Advent sermon. How do you lose interest in a season when the whole point is eager anticipation?

It's true, though—if you've heard the sermon or Scripture or song before, your mind can wander. Even in this series, if we wander through a text or topic you're familiar with, you might want to start skimming. But stay with me!

Our text this week, shown above, is likely a familiar one; it's popular during Advent but also pops up throughout the year. So if you're like I was in middle school and high school, you've already checked off the Scripture box and probably even summed up your own mini-devotional on Jesus setting us free so that we can set others free. But context is everything.

Keep in mind that Jesus is speaking these words. Another layer down reveals that Jesus is actually reading, and the words belong to Isaiah. But before we go any deeper, I want you to feel the change in the atmosphere that is about to occur in the room where Jesus is reading.

When I was in middle school, the pastor of my family's church resigned. He'd had an affair with the high school daughter of a church member. It was a Southern Baptist church, and the girl's father happened to be the chairman of the deacons. An electrifying tale, no doubt. I'm sure some of the key church leadership knew before we did, but most of the congregation found out when a letter from the pastor to the deacon in question was read aloud from the pulpit.

Did your chest tighten a little just then? I can remember the air leaving the room. There was the uncomfortable image of a man in a leadership role having to admit a wound to the congregation that deeply, deeply affected him personally. The tension was palpable. A sense of normalcy didn't return for weeks.

Why am I putting you through my painful memory in an Advent series? Because, believe it or not, the feeling of tension I just described is about to descend on the room where Jesus is reading. How can a text about Jesus coming to set us free bring such turmoil to the crowd? Let's go back to that room.

Free Indeed

It's the Sabbath. Luke records Jesus returning to Galilee from his temptation in the desert, ready to start his ministry. He travels to Nazareth, the town of his childhood. The picture painted by the author of Luke suggests great familiarity with Jesus' presence in the synagogue; clearly he grew up in this community. Jesus stands to read; someone hands him the scroll of Isaiah. All normal so far.

> The Spirit of the Lord is upon me,
>   because the Lord has anointed me.
> He has sent me to preach good news to the poor,
>   to proclaim release to the prisoners
>   and recovery of sight to the blind,
>   to liberate the oppressed,
>   and to proclaim the year of the Lord's favor.
> (Luke 4:18-19 CEB)

Good work, Jesus. Thanks for reading. Some of the listeners have probably actually tuned in for a little while. But then Jesus adds this:

"Today, this scripture has been fulfilled just as you heard it" (v. 21).

Insert mic-drop thump or record-needle scratch. What did that kid just say?

Then Jesus lets them have it. He tells them they would beg him to do miracles. He tells them they will never accept him because he is *from* here. He says that in Elijah's time there were plenty of widows in Israel who were in need of assistance, and God sent Elijah elsewhere to minister. He says there had been plenty of Israelites with leprosy in need of healing, but God chose to heal outsiders instead.

What is so offensive about Jesus' words? What turns that room from happy worshipers to a raging mob? Jesus has observed, pointedly, that an unjust situation is being ignored. The poor only have bad news; he is bringing good. People are being held captive; he is bringing release. Sight to the blind. The oppressed set free. In short, these things wouldn't be necessary if the hearers had already been participating in the movement of God.

In Advent, we're anticipating an uncomfortable Messiah—calling us to join the kingdom movement, urging us to set people free.

Going Deeper

Set Free

When considering the idea of freedom, it's easy to think only of our own freedom. It takes a step beyond that to consider how our freedom might affect others. We're a consuming culture. You will increasingly find that you have money to spend however you want. You may have already started your first job, or you might have saved up from birthdays and other holidays.

It's yours to spend, right?

Read 1 Corinthians 10:23-24.

With online shopping becoming increasingly convenient, the shopper reigns supreme. But are low prices and free two-day shipping the only considerations? Think about these questions before your next purchase:

- Who created this item? What are their working conditions?
- Why am I buying this? Is this the best use of my money?
- Do I need this? Why do I want it?

No Longer Slaves

It can be a little uncomfortable reading about slavery in Scripture. Slavery is often used as a metaphor for spiritual bondage, particularly in the New Testament letters of Paul. Slavery is not yet completely eradicated in our world, but in Paul's time it was so common that it served as a convenient image for the impossible, oppressive hold that sin can have on our spiritual being.

Read Galatians 5:1 (NRSV).

- What do you think Paul means by the phrase "for freedom Christ has set us free"?

In this passage, Paul refers to the fact that early Jewish Christians insisted that Gentiles who believed in the way of Jesus be circumcised as a part of their conversion. Paul felt this was silly. Why would Jesus free us from all of the law only to put us back under part of it?

- What extra conditions have you tried to add to what Jesus asks of us? Do you feel free in following Jesus, or restricted?

Freedom Rules

So we're set free. Awesome! Sounds like do-what-you-want time, right? Not so fast.

Any real freedom comes with guidelines, even if they're self-imposed. Riding a bike brings enormous freedom to kids (and late-adopting adults), but if you try to ignore the laws of balance and gravity while expressing that newfound freedom, you're going to bleed.

Read James 1:22-25.

- Have you ever tried to memorize something in a hurry and realized that you weren't succeeding because you were in a rush? How is that like someone who looks in a mirror and forgets his or her own face?
- In this passage, what does it mean to persevere? If liberty is freedom, how does being "doers of the word"—following biblical guidelines—free us?

Making It Personal

In your devotional time this week, focus on where you're answering God's call on your life to set others free. Truly following in the way of Jesus is guaranteed to be challenging—it involves less of us, and more of him. The process of emptying ourselves of *ourselves* can be daunting. You probably won't experience a Christlike moment of having the entire congregation rise to chase you out of town, but really living like Jesus will likely involve butting heads with someone somewhere.

It's okay to be nervous. It's not hard to imagine that in the synagogue that day, Jesus' first couple of words from the Isaiah passage caught in his throat.

Spend some time this week with these questions:

- Where do I feel God tugging, pushing, maybe even shoving me into action? Am I willing, or resistant?
- How can I let go of my fears about diving in to the freedom of a life like Christ's? What am I afraid of?

Sharing Thoughts and Feelings

Spend some time with the group discussing these questions:

- What is the craziest thing you can remember happening during a church service?
- In the extended passage from Luke (4:16-30), why do you think Jesus chose to be so confrontational? Why not just leave after his eyebrow-raising claim to have personally fulfilled the Scripture? What was he hoping to accomplish by provoking the listeners?
- How does our group encourage each other to be "set free" by God? Be specific.
- What things tend to trip us up or trap us in our daily lives? What things compromise our spiritual freedom?
- In what ways and from what things have you been freed in the time you've known God?

Doing Things Together

Reading the Small Print

Supplies: Sheet of posterboard; markers

Identify one freedom that your group holds in common and would like to discuss. The particular freedom can vary depending on the age of your group. Later bedtimes, greater access to technology, getting learner's permits or driver's licenses—all these freedoms bring new opportunities and challenges in your life. Generally speaking, the freedoms come with increased responsibilities.

When you've chosen a freedom to discuss, spend a few minutes writing on posterboard some of the guidelines or restrictions that come with that freedom. If you're talking about mobile phones, what are your limitations? If it's a car, what rules are you expected to abide by? Does your freedom involve expectations beyond your family's? Are there actual laws involved in that freedom?

How has your group's understanding of spiritual freedom evolved over time? Individual answers are great here. What have you learned from each other?

The Power of Freedom

Supplies: Map of your community; posterboard; markers

We've focused a lot on our own freedom. Let's spend some time focusing on how we as Christians are sent to free others. Dissect the verses from Isaiah that Jesus quotes in Luke 4:18-19 (NRSV). On your posterboard, write these headings:

- Good news to the poor
- Release to the prisoners
- Sight to the blind
- Liberate the oppressed

Now think—*really* think. Where in your community do you see these needs? Take them one at a time. Answer these questions as a group:

- Who are the poor in your community? Where are they?
- What would good news be to them? How can your group bring that good news?

31

- The term *prisoners* sounds like *captives*, but think about other forms of imprisonment.
- What situations, circumstances, or habits imprison people you know?
- What would free them? Can you participate in that?

God probably hasn't equipped you to heal physical blindness, but you may be able to help heal some kinds of mental or experiential blindness.

- What kinds of mental or experiential blindness do you encounter at school or in your community?
- How has God uniquely equipped your group to bring "sight" in those situations?

Oppression takes many forms. You probably have groups of people around you who have had to deal with prolonged, unfair circumstances in some form.

- Who do you know who doesn't have an equal voice?
- Where can your group listen to the needs of people who haven't been heard?

Listening for God

God, we're so grateful that Jesus was sent to free us! May we have the courage to allow ourselves to be sent as well, to be co-laborers in your freeing work. Amen.

3.

JESUS IS GOD WITH US

*"The virgin will conceive and give birth to a son, and
they will call him Immanuel" (which means "God with us").*
(Matthew 1:23 NIV)

Silent Night

A little transparency about the book you're holding in your hand:

Chances are you're reading this during the season of Advent. The night air outside is cool and crisp. You've got a headful of the holidays and whatever that looks like for you and your friends and family. As your writer, I'm somewhere else entirely. Right now it's late June. I'm reading themes and background passages of Scripture and forecasting myself into an Advent mindset—even though in a few hours I'm headed to the pool with my kids.

What that means for the writing process is that I usually have to swing through a couple of theme-based ideas before landing on one that I feel Christmas-y about. But at this instant on this day, for this passage and this theme I'm stuck in a place far from Christmas. However, instead of pressing on to some other angle, I'd like to bring you to where I am. If you'll indulge me, come back to June for a moment.

On June 17, 2015, a young white man attended a Wednesday night Bible study at a Charleston church. Before walking out the door an hour later, he rose and killed nine people. His confessed intention was to start a race war. All nine of his victims were black, including the pastor, who also served as a state senator. The name of the church is Emanuel African Methodist Episcopal Church, referred to as "Mother Emanuel" by its members.

Emanuel, God With Us

Hearing about the shooting, suddenly my Advent spirit's knees buckled a little. The hope and promise of "God with us" at Christmas gave way to a desperate need for God with us right here in June. Where, in fact, was God in this? Senseless killing never finds explanation. Racism is an unhealed, ugly wound in our country. Some respond in anger. Incredibly, the families of those who were killed responded with forgiveness. After a week, it finally occurred to me. Where was God? Right there in the room. It was hardly solace, but in the killer's confession he indicated that, in the end, he almost didn't do it. He realized how nice they all were. But then he did it anyway.

When we think of the presence of God, there's usually some other action attached to it in our minds. God is with us—equipping us, helping us. God is with us—providing. But in this moment, we see God in the most essential part of presence. God was in the room. God was with those people as it happened. God grieved for the loss of life and for the broken child who took them. God was present.

My mom died while I was in college. It's been more than twenty years now, so my memories of the weeks and months surrounding her death are less distinct than they once were. I do remember calling my buddy Keith, my best friend to this day. We no longer lived in the same city, but his response was instant and unexpected: "When can I come?" It hadn't occurred to me that he might. It was my first real loss as an adult. I didn't have any experience to base expectations on. Looking back, I realize that today, years later, I still wouldn't expect it. The offer of a non-family member to drop everything in the name of companionship was unique. I didn't need help with anything; I didn't have any obligations in my mom's arrangements. But he came.

I was still living at home, so Keith slept on my floor for a week. I was working at Office Depot and taking night classes for college, but I had bereavement time off from work and... well, I think I just blew off school that week. I don't remember what we did. There was a lot of IBC cream soda at night. Mostly we just hung out and talked. Not about mom so much, just talked. He was just there. No agenda, not trying to fix anything—just there.

When I look at what happened in Charleston, that's how I see God there. Present, without any other expectation. Sure, it's nice to imagine God stepping in to prevent the killings, but we're not promised the absence of evil. Just God in the room. God with us. Immanuel at Mother Emanuel.

Where We Are

Matthew works the hardest of the four Gospels in the New Testament to connect Jesus to Old Testament texts. Why? Because for the writer of Matthew, our Old Testament was his only testament.

This week's text in Matthew originally appeared in Isaiah 7:14. In its first appearance, these words were delivered by the prophet Isaiah to King Ahaz, who was seeking some good news from the prophet of God. Isaiah told him that a child would be born to a young woman; by the time the kid is old enough to choose between good and bad things, the military threat facing Ahaz will be gone. The name of the child—Immanuel in this version—meant "God with us." The child was born to be a sign of the continuing presence of and relationship with God.

Matthew, seeking to echo that presence, lifts from Isaiah's original words to Ahaz a deeper, distantly prophetic message: Again a child will be born. Again the child shall be called Immanuel. A reminder, again, that God is with us. Among us.

In Advent, we celebrate that approaching presence. Jesus was sent to be with us and to offer us a place with him. May we be with each other as he is with us!

Going Deeper

Presence

The psalms are full of references to God's presence. Sometimes they clamor for God's presence, seeking it when God feels absent. As often as they seek, they rejoice in the wonder of God's attentiveness. David's psalms particularly display his heart on his sleeve when it comes to seeking God's presence. It's fitting, then, that at Pentecost, Peter quoted David while addressing the bewildered crowd. After establishing that the disciples weren't drunk (it had been suggested), he revealed that even death couldn't keep God's presence from us.

Read Acts 2:14-28.

In those final two verses, David (by way of Peter) speaks about being full of gladness due to God's presence.

- When have you experienced God's presence in a moving way?
- Have you ever felt separated from God? What were the circumstances? What was the outcome?
- If you feel separated from God right now, do you have someone you can confide in? Not to "fix" you; just to be with you. When we struggle, it helps to struggle together.

Companions for the Journey

Probably obvious, but Paul didn't have Facebook.

Can you imagine if he did, though? How different would our Scriptures be if Paul had the constant contact of social media? Not many of his sentences fit the 160-character template. Our New Testament contains remnants of the communication method of the day—letters. Actual letters, written by hand, then sent—not by postal carrier, mind you—to their intended church communities. Eventually.

Paul's introductions and conclusions (and a lot of what went between) express his longing for being present at the churches.

Read 1 Corinthians 16:5-12.

Paul doesn't really know when he'll get to Corinth or how long he'll be able to stay. He just wants to be there.

- When have you longed to be near a loved one but for some reason weren't able to be?
- How have you been able to provide presence for someone else in need?
- When you've been separated from someone for a time, how do you stay in contact?

From Beginning to End

We find Jesus at the end of Matthew right where we found him at the beginning—with us. Jesus is revealed in Matthew 1:23 as Immanuel, God with us. In chapter 28, at the very end of Matthew's Gospel, Jesus promises to be with his disciples, even to the end of the age.

Read Matthew 28:16-20.

Matthew's Gospel ends without Jesus really leaving.

- What do you make of that?
- How do you imagine events play out after these verses?

Put yourself in the shoes of a disciple for a moment: there have been tumultuous days leading up to this passage.

- How do you feel as Jesus explains what he wants you to do?
- What does it mean to you that he is "with you always"?

Making It Personal

What was your first moment of being aware of God's presence?

The ways and places that we can encounter God are virtually limitless. This week, make a special effort to be *with* God. If you haven't already found one, designate a physical place you have daily access to as sacred space. You don't have to build a sanctuary, but find a way to consecrate it as a meeting place for you and God. It doesn't even have to be anywhere private; a bench in a park, a corner of the library at school, or anywhere you regularly find yourself will do just fine.

Make time to be in that space each day, even if it's only for a few moments. Pray. Read Scripture. Breathe out your concerns and joys to God. You'll come away refreshed and invigorated. Consider these questions while you're there:

- What new places did I see God this week?
- How am I being God's presence to others?

Don't forget that God is still with you when you go!

Sharing Thoughts and Feelings

Spend some time with the group discussing these questions:

- What is your favorite way that the group celebrates "God with us" during Advent?
- Do you struggle to feel God's presence during Advent or other times of the year? What do you do when God feels distant?
- How do you make sense of God's presence when disaster strikes?
- How do you prepare to welcome God during Advent?
- Does your family have any special practices or traditions during Advent that you could share with the group?

Doing Things Together

See You Later

Supplies: Blindfold

Have a volunteer put on a blindfold and sit in a chair with hands held out in front. Ask two or three people from your group to approach silently and place their hands on the hands of the blindfolded person. The blindfolded person feels the hands of each standing person, then guesses whose hands they are.

After each round, repeat with a new blindfolded person. You can either let everyone participate or play to a winner—most correct guesses wins a…(Prizes not included with book. This is Advent, not Christmas!)

When you're done playing, discuss these questions:

- When you were trying to guess whose hands you were touching, did you use any senses besides your sense of touch? How did that go?
- What are the things you appreciate with your senses when you're in the presence of a loved one? Beyond the five physical senses, what intangible things do you appreciate about being present with them?
- How does this activity relate to how you enjoy God's presence in your life?

Being There

Supplies: List of recently absent church members

There are dozens of reasons people aren't able to attend church with the rest of their Christian community. Some are hospitalized on a short- or long-term basis. Some are physically unable to come from home or lack transportation to do so. Some may be employed at a job that requires them to work during church times.

Get a list from your church office of members who currently are unable to attend services. Work as a group to plan visits to these members in groups of two or three. Whatever the members' reasons for being away, your group can provide the connection of presence that's such a meaningful part of being in the body of Christ. Any reminder of that connection that we can offer to others is important, especially during Advent.

Where appropriate, try to find ways to bring these people to services during the Advent and Christmas holidays. Transportation is an obstacle that can usually be overcome, and sometimes people have just fallen out of the habit of attending. Be invitational!

Listening for God

God, we welcome your presence at Advent. We're so grateful that you sent Jesus to be with us. We need you here so much! Help us to embrace opportunities to extend your presence to others as Christmas approaches. Amen.

4.

JESUS BRINGS NEW LIFE

The hand of the LORD was on me, and he brought me out by the Spirit of the LORD and set me in the middle of the valley; it was full of bones. . . . He asked me, "Son of man, can these bones live?" I said, "Sovereign LORD, you alone know." Then he said to me, "Prophesy to these bones and say to them, 'Dry bones, hear the word of the LORD!'" . . . So I prophesied as I was commanded. And as I was prophesying, there was a noise, a rattling sound, and the bones came together, bone to bone. (Ezekiel 37:1, 3-4, 7 NIV)

The Valley of Bones

I've read this passage from Ezekiel many, many times in my life. It's one of those that you keep coming back to, and almost every time I do I read it a little differently. I can remember as a kid being fascinated with the mental image of an entire valley filled with scattered, jumbled bones. The imagined rumble of skeletons snapping back together. Terrifying, in a way.

I remember approaching the text again in college, this time seeing the valley at peace. The bones were so far beyond life, the view was serene, not grisly. Death no longer entered the scene. No smell. No scavengers. Just old bones, baking in the sun. I was especially taken with the absurdity of the idea that the bones would come back to life. I could imagine Ezekiel's reply: "I mean, I guess you could make them live again, God, but...why bother?"

The next time I came back to the passage, it was me standing in the valley, living out Ezekiel's vision.

On April 26, 2011, a tornado ripped the heart out of Ringgold, the small north Georgia town where my family served a local United Methodist church. In one of the most vicious tornado seasons on record, our little community began a new journey together as we wrestled with devastating loss.

To the outside world, the town of Ringgold exists primarily as the "food exit." If you're traveling south toward Atlanta, we're the place where you've just cleared Chattanooga and are ready for a break. If you're traveling north from Atlanta, you haven't seen restaurants or gas in many miles, so you also come to see us.

It was a Wednesday night, and our pastor had canceled our church's evening activities as a "just in case" against a severe weather forecast. It was the best call of his ministry career, though he didn't know it at the time. If we'd had church that night, we'd have been standing in the parking lot when the tornado hit.

As it was, I went home and sat on my couch. We were watching NetFlix and keeping tabs on the weather by looking out the window. At the time we didn't have a real plan for bad weather. Our 1930s farmhouse didn't offer much in the way of storm-proof structure.

We were actually standing in the yard as the tornado began. It formed right above us and began to drag destructive fingers less than a mile away as it headed toward town. When it reached the highway, the real havoc began. The tornado flung vehicles from the bridge, then demolished nearly every restaurant and business in its path to the high school and middle school. After having its way with those, it hopped the ridge and came down with deadly force in a residential area.

The weeks that followed were, at the very least, heartbreaking. Law enforcement set up a perimeter, initially closing the town to anyone other than first responders and rescue workers. After three days—by permit only—our church staff was allowed back in. I cringed when I saw our church. It was nearly pristine. Not a window broken. We found minor damage here and there, eventually requiring replacement of the roof and repair of a structural beam in the sanctuary, but for the most part we were untouched.

Why cringe, you ask? Because a restaurant twenty yards from our gym was leveled. Because the office of the Division of Family and Children Services was gutted, with private documents scattered to the wind. Because the last thing I wanted was for anyone in our community to think that God had protected a church building while letting everything else get blown to smithereens.

If you haven't experienced it firsthand, it's difficult to describe seeing your everyday surroundings crunched up and stacked in piles everywhere you look. Nothing made sense. Massive steel I-beams laced around trees like pipe cleaners. A church van flipped onto its crushed roof with a "Please Do Not Block Drive" sign stuck into its rear wheel well. A bathtub found in the principal's office at the high school.

Can these bones live? Oh, Lord God, you know.

To Bring New Life

Our valley of bones did spring back to life. It was incredible to watch. Power companies from several states came together and replaced the electrical nervous system of our town in a matter of days, including every single power pole being switched for a new one. Our church, because it was standing and because our people cared, became the hub of volunteer efforts. Crews came from across the country. The stage in our gym was converted into a dormitory for rotating Mennonite groups who came to help, coordinated through our temporary relief office. We would never have asked for it, but we were able to play a key role in bringing new life to our community.

Jesus was sent to bring new life. The valley of dry bones that he encountered did not lay scattered where the naked eye could see them. Jesus came to bring life to different dry bones, the spiritual kind that once had resonated with the love of God and neighbor. Jesus was sent to restore the relationship between God and God's people, and—miraculously—to extend that relationship to the entire world.

Can these bones live? Oh, Lord God, you know.

So what's our call here? How are we to participate in being sent? This Advent, ask God to show you the dry bones around you. You may already be walking in a place that needs healing and not even have realized it.

Going Deeper

Light in the Darkness

We have what I consider a bad habit when it comes to quoting Scripture. We lift super-positive verses with the intention of affirmation. But, removed from their context and posted on Facebook or happy Christian merchandise such as T-shirts, posters, and the occasional cross-stitch project, these verses can give the impression that our Scripture is mostly cheery good news, and therefore largely irrelevant during difficult times. If I'm feeling low, I must be out of step with Scripture. Right? Nope.

Read Lamentations 3:1-23.

Whoa. Hard times, huh? But that last verse may have seemed familiar; it's the happy part, after all. ("Great is your faithfulness.") The writer of Lamentations is doing some serious lemonade-out-of-lemons footwork here.

- What's the most difficult time you can remember in your faith journey? Where were you able to find light in the dark?
- Have there been times when you felt completely overcome? How did you move forward?
- What about Advent speaks to you about new life?

When All Is Lost

One of the most amazing things about Jesus coming to bring new life is that a lot of people didn't understand what he was here to do. In this chapter, we've seen some very real examples of loss and restoration. The people Jesus came to restore—even his chosen disciples—didn't get his message, for the most part, until after he was gone. If he was going to restore anything, they had thought it would be the kingdom of Israel. But Jesus' kingdom wasn't about the government. Jesus' kingdom was about changing hearts and restoring the law of love.

Read Job 1:13-22.

- How could Job bless God in the face of such sudden, traumatic loss?
- What is your instinctive response to God when you face loss?
- Do you have previous valley experiences that you haven't allowed to heal?

In the story of Job, most of the rest of the book is devoted to bad advice from well-intentioned friends.

- When you're aware that someone is in need of restoration, how can you be a life-bringing presence?
- This Advent, what part of you is waiting to be revived into new life?

It's All or Nothing at All

We don't have to experience death—figurative or literal—to have new life available to us. Like the disciples and early Christians, we can realize that a different kind of life is all the new life we need. New life doesn't mean getting everything we want or even everything we think we might need. The kind of new life we prepare to receive during Advent is transformation. Jesus is our life. Not in a hokey, church-answer kind of way. Jesus is sufficient. Everything else is just the circumstance in which we will live our new life.

Read Philippians 4:12-13.

Paul's lifestyle wasn't for the faint of heart. In and out of prison, loved by some and not by others, perpetually on the road facing danger and criticism, Paul surely longed for home and stability from time to time. In this letter, however, he hints that he has found a different definition of contentedness that has nothing to do with where he's staying, what he's eating, or whom he's with.

- How much do you let circumstances dictate your happiness?
- What things do you consider keys to your life—what can't you live without?
- Do you come to Advent this year contented, or are you longing for something different in life?

Making It Personal

Wherever you are on your journey with God, it's a sacred place. If this is the first experience you've had with God or the church, welcome to the way! If you're farther along the path, you've probably experienced some ups and downs already. It's the nature of trying to live in relationship with God; we'll succeed at times and seem to fail at others—but it's all part of the process.

During Advent, we revisit the miracle that Jesus was sent to bring us new life—continually revitalizing our weary dry bones.

This week, write a few letters of thanks to people who have helped guide you on your journey.

- Who was there at the beginning?
- Whose are the first supportive Christian voices you remember?

Just a simple card with a few simple thoughts will do. Your thanks will mean more to those people than you could ever believe.

Sharing Thoughts and Feelings

Spend some time with the group discussing the following questions:

- Has your group ever had a "valley experience"? What happened? How did the group find new life?
- What are the some of the changes you've seen when new life comes to your group?
- Have you ever missed an opportunity to participate in bringing new life to others? What were the circumstances?

- Did any stories come up during your reading this week that you would like to share?
- What signs of new life in your church or community have you seen this Advent?

Doing Things Together

From the Ashes

Supplies: Paper and pens (with a little work ahead of time!)

Before your group meets this week, have a volunteer contact a local fire station or emergency services department to find a family who recently suffered property loss. It's possible that your church office staff may know of someone and be able to save you the search. Get a list of names, ages, and clothing sizes.

When your group meets, brainstorm a list of creature comforts that those people might not be thinking of at the moment—books to read, games to play, and so on. Contact a local thrift store about gathering items for the family. The store might donate the items, but if not, you could collect money from your group and go shopping—benefiting the family and the store!

Tell the family that you've been talking during Advent about how Jesus was sent to bring new life to us—and that you're excited for the opportunity to help bring some new life to them.

You may want to enlist help from the rest of your church. Consider putting an announcement in the church bulletin or signs in the hallway. Be sure to state clearly the needs and a designated drop-off time and date.

Celebrating New Life

Supplies: List of babies born this year in your church (and their families)

What better way to celebrate new life during Advent than actually *celebrating new life*? Using a list of newborns, brainstorm a list of items to put in Christmas bags for each of the families, then go shopping as a group.

As much as possible, tailor the bags to the individual family. Some items can be common to all the gift bags, but make sure you also plan what would be meaningful to each family. When you have the bags ready, set aside an evening or two to deliver them personally.

Listening for God

God, we recognize the need for new life within us. Thank you so much for sending Jesus to bring that life to us! All of us walk through different valleys at different times in our lives. Help us to be aware of people who need us to walk alongside them. We love you and welcome you at Advent! Amen.

5.

JESUS CHANGES EVERYTHING

When the time was just right, God sent his Son, born of a woman.... (Galatians 4:4a NLT)

Time to Get to Work

A few years ago I worked as a carpenter in some wealthy neighborhoods of Atlanta. How wealthy? Our French doors were sometimes actually shipped from France. It wasn't uncommon for us to complete a project only to have the homeowner say, "Nah, do it again differently," knowing full well their cost would double.

The running joke among our crew was that some people draw with pencils, and some people draw with carpenters. Price was no object, and at times I would feel a little ill about the amounts of money being spent on things that didn't really matter. Like the time we installed a $96,000 front door. Yep, just for the door. It was a double door, fifteen feet tall and four feet wide with windows made of onyx—stone shaved so thin that light could pass through. Crazy.

My job was usually site supervisor, scheduling and overseeing framing and sheet-rock crews or plumbers and electricians. My personal specialty was trim work, installing doors, windows, elaborate crown molding, and baseboards. Occasionally there would be a job large enough that I went to work under another site supervisor and just installed trim. I loved those jobs, because it meant that for a few days or weeks, the pressure of responsibility came off of me and went onto someone else.

One guy I worked with was like a legend among us. Roger had been a master carpenter in Ireland before moving to the United States. He worked harder, faster, and better than any two of us put together. He would always be the first to arrive and the last to leave. We called him "the Irish Kid" even though he was older than all of us. Anytime I heard I'd be working with him, I would experience a sense of dread and awe; I was amazed to watch him work but also intimidated, because I felt so useless next to him.

One day I was running trim on another supervisor's project. I had been arriving on time every morning, but the other supervisor, whose name was Rick, had the keys and was nearly always late, so I'd been starting each day with a nap of at least an hour. When I pulled up that morning to an empty driveway, I put my truck in park and slouched down in the seat, leaning my head against the doorjamb. After a few minutes I realized I was hearing something, a persistent whining. Could it be a table saw?

Just as I realized it was in fact a table saw, Roger emerged from the door that I had presumed was locked. I got out of the truck. "Is Rick here?" I asked.

"No," answered Roger with his usual gruff brevity. He started down the driveway to where his truck had been parked out of sight.

"But, Roger," I called after him, "how did you get in?"

He stopped and looked back. "I kicked through the plywood."

As a part of this particular renovation, three new sets of French doors were being installed on the back of the house. The doors hadn't arrived yet, so in the meantime—for security and to keep the weather out—we had installed plywood over the openings.

"You kicked through the *plywood*?" I repeated in disbelief. "Why would you do that?"

"It was time to get to work," he said. Then turned on his heel and marched off.

It's More Than Just Showing Up

Roger's work ethic clearly ran a little deeper than mine. While I was dozing in my truck and Roger was using the table saw, we were both on the clock. We were both drawing pay from the same boss. I was, arguably, at work. I had arrived; I was on time. But I was waiting for someone else to show up before doing anything. Not Roger. If it was time to work, Roger would kick through any and all obstacles to begin the task at hand. That simply had never occurred to me.

In the same way, it's easy to arrive at our professed faith every morning and fail to get out of the truck.

56

After all, we're present and accounted for, right? We've said the right things and believed the right things. During Advent, we've gotten excited about this Jesus who was sent to reconcile, set us free, be with us, and bring new life. Jesus is terrific. But Jesus has shown up with a different attitude than we have. Jesus isn't waiting for somebody to show up with a key. Jesus kicked down the plywood. And Jesus wants us to join him.

Going Deeper

Jesus Reconciles

Reread the text from Luke 2, and this time read verses 8-20.

- What would have happened if the shepherds had stayed put? The angels didn't actually *say* the shepherds had to go. Would anything have changed if they didn't participate?
- Looking back, have you had opportunities to participate in God's story that you've let pass? What were they? What could you have done?
- What does it mean in your life to be reconciled to God? How can you participate in being sent to reconcile in the world around you?

Jesus Sets Us Free

Reread the text from Luke 4, and this time read verses 16-30.

- What was so upsetting to the people in the synagogue?
- How do you think that incident may have been freeing for Jesus?
- Have you ever felt called to do something uncomfortable in response to God? What was it? What made it uncomfortable?
- What's your natural response to doing something that stretches your faith? Do you usually go through with it, or do you shy away from the opportunity?
- How is God sending you to set others free?

Jesus Is God With Us

Reread the text from Matthew 1, and this time read verses 18-23.

- What does it mean for God to be "with you"? What difference does it make in your faith for God to come in human form?
- What opportunities have you had to be the presence of God to someone else? How does it make you feel when you realize what's going on? Is it challenging? fulfilling? scary? awesome?
- How do you see God being with us today?
- Is God's presence with us something you're able to point out to others? How do you do that?

Jesus Brings New Life

Reread the text from Ezekiel 37, and this time read verses 1-14.

- What new images did you see while reading the passage this time?
- What dry, dead places can you identify in your own experience where you'd like God to bring new life?
- Have you had experiences with your group or individually where you were able to help bring new life to someone in your church? in your community?
- Are you willing to ask God specifically for opportunities to do that?

Sharing Thoughts and Feelings

Spend some time with the group discussing these questions:

- What are your big takeaways from this series?
- How has your understanding of Jesus changed in the last few weeks?
- What have you learned about your role in the movement of God?
- What new things are you looking forward to incorporating in your faith journey as a result of the time you've spent here?

Doing Things Together

Catching Up

If conversation between your group and an adult group hasn't been part of the last few weeks of this series, now is the time!

Talk with the leaders of any adult groups that have been using the *Sent* book. Arrange a night to get together in the next couple of weeks. Plan a shared meal, then talk through the main themes of this book. Their book had different stories, but the Scriptures and themes were the same.

Plan in advance what you'd like to learn from your time with their group, and be prepared to share your group's experiences, too. One starting point might be to use the questions above, under each chapter topic.

Listening for God

God, we celebrate every opportunity to be with your people during Advent. Thank you for coming into our midst! We're grateful for your reconciling work. We could not live without your freedom. We need you here with us. And we thrive in the new life you provide. Gracious God, we thank you. Amen.

Kevin Alton

is a youth worker, writer, musician, husband, father, and friend. He lives and works near Chattanooga, Tennessee, and is a regular contributor to youth resources, including YouthWorker Movement and his own Wesleyan resouce for curriculum and community, Youthworker Circuit (www.youthworkercircuit.com).